GAME FARMING
FOR
PROFIT AND PLEASURE

A MANUAL

on the wild turkeys, grouse, quail or
partridges, wild ducks and the introduced
pheasants and gray partridges; with special reference to their food, habits, control
of natural enemies and the best methods
of preserving and breeding; including, also,
an appendix on powder, loads, etc.,

by

the author of
"OUR FEATHERED GAME"

Fully illustrated with photographs
and many original drawings
by
Clement B. Davis

19 © 15
BY

HERCULES POWDER CO.
Wilmington Del. U.S.A.

i

FOREWORD

THIS little book is offered to the people of North America in the hope that it will hasten the day when our continent shall produce enough game to supply abundant food, and health giving recreation.

The author predicts that America will eventually be the greatest game producing country in the world, and we believe he points the logical way for the fulfillment of this prophecy. It is time for us to unite in creating, through our own industry, a wealth of wild life to take the place of that which nature gave us, and we so thoughtlessly destroyed. Heretofore our energies have been mainly expended in trying to bring back the game by prohibitory legislation. Our laws have said, "You must not kill game," instead of "You may raise game." These laws have undoubtedly done much good in a negative way, but they offer no real solution of the problem. They are not creative. Some of them we shall probably need always, but many of them will become obsolete shortly after laws permitting game breeding are enacted. Prohibitions which seem important when there is little game to protect will become superfluous when a large supply is constantly maintained.

In promoting game breeding, the Hercules Powder Company naturally considers its own interests, but fortunately they are inalienably linked with the country's welfare in this important matter. We feel no hesitancy in asking all sportsmen who believe our efforts are in the right direction, to support them by giving us their patronage.

We take pleasure in acknowledging our indebtedness to

the American Museum of Natural History for photographs and drawings made from its collections.

Hand Thrown Books

West Newbury, MA

Antiquarian Reprints
This softbound edition reproduces
"Game Farming"
as published in 1915 by the Hercules Powder Company
in an effort to bring antiquarian sporting books to a wider audience than could
possibly be reached by access only to those remaining copies of the originally
published works
Special contents of this edition copyright 2013

CONTENTS

Restoration 1

Game Enemies 7

The Wild Turkey 13

American Quails & Partridge 19

Bob White 27

The Grouse of the
        Open Country 31

The Prairie Grouse 37

The Grouse of the
        Woods and Mountains 45

Ruffed Grouse 49

Wild Ducks 54

The Pheasants 61

The Gray Partridge 67

Appendix 69

NORTH AMERICA had, only, few years ago, a greater number and variety of valuable wild food birds than any Country in the world. The records of two guns shooting, with muzzle-loaders, over a hundred wood-cock in a day, quite near New York; of the shooting of over a hundred bay snipe at a single discharge; of the shooting of wagon loads of prairie grouse and wild ducks, seem incredible, but they are authentic as recorded in our ornithologies. Bogardus tells us that with a friend he shot three hundred and forty Wilson's snipe one day, in Illinois, and Mr. Pringle, in his history of "The Snipery," in Louisiana, records the taking of thousands of these toothsome birds during a season, hooting day after day over marshes near the house. Cody (Buffalo Bill) records the killing of four or five hundred wild turkeys at one camp in the West. The placing of a bounty on the ruffed grouse, in Massachusetts, because it was considered too abundant for the successful growing of fruit; the destruction of prairie grouse, in Kentucky, because, as Audubon says, they were regarded as pests, and many more

1

recent records might be cited to prove the former great abundance of our true game birds of the upland and our wild fowl and waders. The writer was present one day, in Ohio, when the bag contained over a hundred and fifty quail besides ruffed grouse and wood-cock, and a few wood duck and miscellaneous birds and rabbits for good measure. The bags always were large although we shot day after day over a comparatively small area.

Our ornithologists and sporting writers deplore the rapid disappearance of this wonderful food supply and often they predict the extermination of game in America. Some recommend, continually, more stringent game laws, limiting or prohibiting sport, but, since the game has continued to vanish notwithstanding such enactments, many have doubted the possibility of saving the more valuable upland species if any shooting be permitted. There is good reason for the doubt. A large and ever increasing number of guns, each taking only a few birds during a short open season, undoubtedly produces the same result which was produced by a smaller number of guns, each taking a larger number of birds during a long open season.

All naturalists agree that the absolute prohibition of field sports does some good only when the species has not been too much decimated to survive its natural enemies. All agree that even a little shooting is too much, unless the game enemies be controlled, because any slight additional check to the increase of a species must cause it rapidly to decrease in numbers. The prohibition of sport, which we have been facing, is highly undesirable. Fortunately we now know that it is unnecessary.

Field sports need no defense or apology in so far as the readers of this little book are concerned. Their enemies do not realize the importance of the health-giving exercise which they denounce or the economic value of the food which field sports can be made to produce. The distinguished ornithologist, Elliot, in his book on our gallinaceous game birds, refers to the pleasure they yield and the incentive they provide for action and effort, "when in the leafy aisles of whispering forests, or in

2

the thickets and along the banks of the leaping stream, or in the open sky-encircled prairie, man in his quest for these game-like creatures, aided by his faithful dog, finds renewed health and strength to wrestle with the toils and troubles of his daily life."

The food value of our game birds becomes more and more important as the prices of beef and mutton continue to rise, as it seems they must, as population increases. The restoration of field sports and the propagation and practical protection of our game birds have become of great economic importance. I am pleased to observe that the tendency of our legislation is in the direction of encouraging the profitable production of game. I firmly believe, with the aid of intelligent State Game Officers, the sportsmen and game farmers of America can make the game birds more plentiful than they ever were, using only a small portion of the lands suitable for game which long have been posted against all shooting. As we shall observe, the natural enemies of game and the dogs and cats, and illegal gunners must be controlled on some of the breeding grounds if field sports are to be perpetuated in America. Since it is absolutely necessary that our game be properly preserved and multiplied on some of the farms with the farmer's consent, I am in favor of it. There is no danger of game preserving being overdone. The country is too big. We should remember, also, that for the most part it must be done on the farms where shooting already is prohibited and that such industry can harm no one.

The area of the public forests and parks in America is said to be larger than the area of Germany. The area of our public waters and marshes, where sport is free to all comers, is many times as big as such areas are in the older countries, where the market gunners are permitted to shoot. Our prejudice against the producers of game has disappeared rapidly and now that we know our game must become extinct if any shooting be permitted and no one looks after its increase, I predict that all prejudice against the producers soon will vanish just as the prejudice against many modern inventions has vanished when it was ascertained to be founded upon an ignorance of the good results soon to follow. In the states where game breeding has been encouraged by legislation there is no longer any objection to such industry. A broiled grouse, properly served, may be made to convert an enemy of sport, and an abundance of game in our markets will make most of the people friendly to those who shoot it. The amount of game which now is being reared throughout the country indicates that good sport soon will be restored for all hands during a long open season, beginning with the prairie grouse in August and ending with the wild fowl before the nesting season in the spring.

All of the grouse and quails or partridges are best reared in a wild state on protected areas. It is by such methods that the European grouse and gray partridges have been made tremendously plentiful everywhere and are kept so although the markets are fully supplied. Wild bred birds are the cheapest, since they find much of their food in the fields. They are more easily reared, since they are more free from diseases than hand-reared birds. They are better for sport on account of their wildness and better for the table on account of their flavor, than the hand-reared birds.

There are two kinds of game keeping and two kinds of game keepers. The best game keepers simply look after the wild breeding birds on the areas or beats assigned to them, usually from 1000 to 1500 acres. They control the enemies of the birds see that their natural covers and foods are adequate and when the game becomes abundant as it will quickly when so protected, additional foods often are provided, especially during the winter. The hand-rearing keepers are similar to poultry rearers. Their methods will be referred to fully in the chapters on the pheasants and the wild ducks which are the birds handled by these keepers.

"Coming Back."

Vermin, the name given to the numerous enemies of game birds, by the English writers and game keepers. Captain D Maxwell, in his book on Partridges, devotes a chapter to vermin and the methods of its control, and the English sporting magazines often give space to stories of the destruction of game by its enemies and the best means for preventing such loss. Until a few years ago the word vermin was not mentioned in our sporting literature, and few sportsmen realized the amount of game destroyed annually by predaceous animals and the absolute necessity for controlling them if we would continue to shoot.

Owen Jones, in "Ten Years of Game Keeping," says: "Let the keeper look after the vermin and the game will look after itself, is a saying which has stood the test of time." Fryer, an authority on gray partridges, tells us the control of vermin "is an all important matter and one that affects the stock even more than the weather at hatching time." Macpherson, in his book on the grouse, says it is necessary to supplement a good supply of food for the grouse by waging war against its four-footed and winged persecutors. Darwin believes that if shooting were stopped in England there would be less game than at present although hundreds of thousands of animals are annually shot. All naturalists are aware that a large number of the game birds and their eggs are destroyed by predaceous animals every year otherwise the game would soon overrun the earth. The tendency to increase is tremendous. It is well known that nature preserves a delicate balance and that if for any reason additional causes of destruction or checks to the increase of any species be added, the species quickly will become reduced in numbers, and that soon it will become extinct, if the check to increase be serious. A little shooting by many guns, for example, surely will put an end to the game if none of the natural enemies be controlled to make a place for the shooting. The converse of the proposition is well stated by Darwin: "Reduce the checks to increase even slightly and the species will increase quickly, to any amount." It is evident why the game remains abundant where it is protected from its enemies and why it vanishes in America, so that, often, it becomes necessary to enact laws prohibiting shooting. I know many game keepers in all parts of America who keep the shooting good because they control the vermin. Thousands of quail can be and are safely shot in places where the hawks, crows, foxes, snakes, weasels, and many other natural enemies are trapped and shot persistently

Horace G. Hutchinson, in writing about the Scotch grouse, said, "The death of one stoat means the life of many grouse." Our prairie grouse are preyed upon by hawks as well as by foxes and many other furry and winged enemies, and skunks take many birds and eggs. The result is we have no grouse shooting.

The woodland grouse, the wild fowl and waders, the partridges or quails, all suffer similar losses and we can not shoot many birds without causing them rapidly to decrease in numbers. The introduced pheasants and partridges suffer even more from vermin than our indigenous birds do, because they come from

8

places where vermin has been steadily controlled, and they are more innocent of the dangers due to lurking foes than our birds are.

1 Crow.
2 Foxes.
3 Coyote.
4 Snapper.
5 Hawk.
6 Black Snake.
7 Skunks.

.Since the necessity for looking after some of the breeding grounds and protecting them from vermin is now apparent it follows that such industry should be encouraged by legislation, as it now is by the game breeders' laws which recently have been enacted in many states. The excellent shooting which the game breeders provide for themselves results in restocking the neighborhood, and game breeding associations have become popular especially those which have small dues and provide good shooting for many guns. It would be impossible here to do more than mention some of the more important game enemies and the methods of their control.

The fox is regarded as a deadly enemy of all ground nesting birds and the game is known to suffer much from this sly animal. I have photographs showing the destruction of ruffed grouse by foxes, on the snow; and the many feathers and bones found in the fox's den indicate that the young foxes are fed on game. Other grouse, quail, partridges, woodcocks and wild fowl are eagerly devoured by the fox.

In the West the coyote and other wolves are very destructive, not only to game birds, but also to deer and antelope. The mountain lion, or cougar, and the lynx are equally destructive.
Minks and weasels hunt wantonly and kill far more game birds than they can eat. There are records of minks killing scores of birds in a night, and only a few days ago I had a report from a breeding ground, in which I am interested, stating that a weasel had destroyed many young pheasants and that rattlesnakes also were eating the young birds. These snakes and black snakes and others not only eat young birds, but they destroy old birds on the nest and devour many eggs. I have seen young pheasants as large as quail taken from snakes which were killed by keepers. A fox terrier is often used to locate snakes and these pests are easily destroyed with a club or gun, when found.

A number of hawks, notably the Coopers hawk, goshawk, and red shouldered hawk, put in much of their time killing and eating game birds and I have observed some of the smaller hawks, which are deemed to be beneficial birds, destroying

10

quail and pheasants. There are records of the duck-hawk hunting wantonly and striking down many ducks during a chase through the air, without stopping to eat them.

The larger owls are fond of game birds and often kill young wild turkeys and other birds roosting in trees. Turtles destroy many young wild ducks and there is a list of many other enemies, all of which do some damage and some of which do great damage at times. Crows are persistent destroyers of young game birds and eggs and I have observed them taking young poultry. Skunks do far more damage; I am sure, than some naturalists are inclined to admit. Farmers, who have observed these animals taking poultry, know that they can take wild birds and their eggs even more easily. The shotgun and many traps are tie remedies used by most game-keepers. The traps used are the ordinary steel traps used to catch minks, weasels, skunks, and other animals, and small round steel traps called pole traps, which are as easily set on poles as the common ground traps are set on the ground. The pole traps should be set on high poles and on the higher branches of the trees which are frequented by hawks and crows. On no account should they be set on low fence posts and in small trees, since they may destroy song birds and I even have known them to kill bob-whites when so placed. The traps can be procured from any hardware store. Some favor the use of poison, which is very fatal, of course, when used with tempting baits. Valuable animals and even people have been killed by poisoned eggs, and the use of poison is no longer approved by many keepers and in some places its use is prohibited.

The cutting down of briars and other protecting covers for the game birds exposes them to their enemies, and in some places the game cannot survive even when shooting is prohibited. Cats, dogs, and rats are added to the list of enemies and tend to upset nature's balance in populous regions. It is very evident that something more than laws limiting the bag and shortening the shooting season is absolutely necessary if field sports are to be perpetuated in America.

Often people may be heard to say that game was abundant when no vermin was destroyed. This is quite true; immense numbers were produced in order to supply the needs of vermin. The birds left were intended to restock the fields and woods. It does not follow that an army of guns can safely shoot these stock birds. The game can stand the losses due to vermin or the losses due to shooting, but not both. In the older countries it survives tremendous losses due to shooting because the vermin is controlled and the birds are properly looked after.

THE restoration and propagation of wild turkeys has become of great economic importance because our domestic turkeys are decimated by a disease, which has made it impossible to rear them on vast areas where turkey breeding was an important industry. Fortunately the wild birds, which are comparatively free from diseases, can be introduced and quickly made abundant in many places throughout their former range, from Southern Maine and Canada to Florida, and westward to Wisconsin and Arizona. The breeding range, no doubt, can be much extended since the wild turkeys have been introduced successfully in California and other Western states.

Our ornithologists recognize four species of wild turkeys: the common wild turkeys of the Eastern states; the Florida turkey, which is somewhat smaller and darker than the Eastern bird; the Elliot's Rio Grande turkey, a handsome species found in the lowlands of Southern Texas and Eastern Mexico; and the Mexican wild turkey (from which came all our domestic turkeys which is distinguished by the light rump with broad white borders to the feathers. But to the sportsman all these forms are alike good game birds when they go whirring through the woods like big ruffed grouse, and all are regarded as far

13

better on the table than the best domestic birds.

Wild turkeys inhabit the forest, but wander out into fields in their search for food, and they can be successfully introduced in farming regions, where the woodlands are not large, provided a number of farms be included in one preserve. The so-called "more game" movement in America has resulted in many experiments with wild turkeys. They have been bred in a wild state on the great quail preserves in North Carolina, where I have seen them nesting quite near farm buildings. Here they are protected from their natural enemies, and from cats and trespassing gunners, by skilled game keepers. In the absence of such care they never could have been restored and in the absence of the keepers, here as elsewhere, they soon would become extinct.

The late Professor Blanton, of Richmond, Virginia, was the first to breed wild turkeys commercially in America, and in an interesting account of wild turkey breeding, written for The Game Breeder's Magazine, he said he hatched some young wild turkeys in a hotel room, using an electric light for his incubator. The Woodmont Rod & Gun Club, of Maryland, has reared large numbers of these birds for sport and had about a thousand turkeys last season. This number easily can be increased. Mr. Bridges, a member of the club, has several hundred wild turkeys on his farm near Baltimore. There are many commercial game farmers and some importers who sell live wild turkeys and their eggs. These have sold wild turkeys which have gone to breeders in the South and as far west as California.

The Game Breeders Association on Long Island, N. Y., made some simple experiments with wild turkeys purchased in Virginia. One hen which nested wild in the woods laid ten eggs which were lifted by a game-keeper and hatched under a barnyard fowl. The turkey persisted in laying and, although her nest was robbed a second time, she brought off a brood of seven or eight birds. Twenty-six eggs were hatched from this bird, which indicates that nature's records easily are beaten when eggs are stolen and young birds are hand-reared. From all the experiments above referred to, the industry of breeding wild turkeys for sport and for profit has received a great impetus and I predict that the markets soon will be filled with cheap wild turkeys since the tendency of sport is to overdo things when it undertakes game breeding.

It is important to keep down the natural enemies of turkeys and to wire the ground enemies out from the rearing fields. Do not make the birds too tame. Turkeys are easily domesticated and when too tame for sport they will probably suffer from the diseases which destroy our tame birds. The laws should not compel the breeding of game birds "in captivity" as some statutes read. The food of young wild turkeys is largely grasshoppers; later they eat berries, and in the autumn and winter acorns and mast of various kinds are the principal food. Acorns are a staple and when plentiful they will keep the turkeys at home and when they fail the turkeys will migrate unless they be properly fed with grain, nuts or other foods. They are very fond of pecans and in the South they eat many of these nuts. Woodlands for food and cover and grassy openings bordering fields for grasshoppers, make ideal ground for wild turkey preserving.

Wild turkeys are now quoted from $15 to 820 for gobblers; $20 to $25 for hens. Turkeys, like other pheasants are polygamous: one gobbler and from three to six hens make the proper groups for breeding. The eggs sell readily at $10 to $12 per dozen. These prices undoubtedly will fall somewhat in a few years; and the prices for turkeys in the markets soon should be lower than the price of domestic
turkeys now is, when some big turkey "shoots" are started in the West and South. Turkeys can be reared cheaply on areas where their natural foods are abundant and sport will pay a good part of the cost of production. Wild turkeys can be successfully introduced, no doubt, on the wild fowl preserves about the Great Lakes and in Canada, where mast bearing woods adjoin the marshes. They have been introduced successfully and are breeding on the state refuges in the Pennsylvania mountains and with proper attention soon they can be made abundant in many places throughout their former range, and in states where they were not indigenous. Doubtless, the destruction of the forests had much to do with the disappearance of the wild turkeys. Elliot ascribes the loss to "too much shooting, chiefly"; but I am inclined to charge it to the lack of practical preservation since the turkeys, like other

game birds, will stand a lot of shooting, provided they be protected from their natural enemies and provided they have suitable covers (even small ones will do) and an abundance of food.

Hen Fostermother with Young Wild Turkeys

OUR American quails or partridges differ in size from the partridges and quails of Europe. They are smaller than the old world partridges, and larger than the little migratory quail. The five genera and thirteen species found in North America are all handsome game birds, excellent in the field and on the table; one of them, the bob-white, I regard as the best game bird in the world.

There are many forms of bob-white, which have been classified as sub-species by the ornithologists. Some of these inhabit Mexico. Within the United States we have two species, the ordinary quail or partridge of the Northern states and the masked or black-throated bob-white which is found in limited numbers in southern Arizona and more abundant in Sonora, Mexico. The sub-species are the Texas bob-white, a somewhat smaller bird and lighter in color than the Northern form and the Florida bobwhite which, is much darker and somewhat smaller than the Northern bob-white. They all, including the masked bob-white, have similar habits, lie well to the dog and equally well on the plate, and they all sound the cheery notes, "Bob-White," in the mating season. Our birds are more similar in their appearance and habits to the European partridges than they are to the old-world' quails^ which are migratory. In Virginia and the South the birds are more often called partridges; in the Northern states they are called quail. The use of the word "quail," however, is becoming common in parts of the South because many Northern men and clubs now have quail preserves in the South, where the shooting is good, always, because the birds are properly looked after. Now that we are introducing the gray partridge of Europe the term quail, applied to our indigenous species, may be useful to distinguish the birds.

The other American quail are the California mountain and valley quail, the Gambel's quail, a bird somewhat similar in size to .the California valley quail, the two forms of the scaled quail and the peculiar Mearn's quail which resembles, somewhat, a little guinea-hen. These Western and Southwestern quail all are handsome birds and they are very good to eat, but often they run before the dogs and they are not, on this account, such desirable objects of pursuit as the bob-white.

Our quail are monogamous. They build their nests on the ground and lay numerous eggs. One pair of any species and its progeny would produce five or six million birds, at a low estimate, in eight years if there were no losses; so that it is evident that these birds quickly can be made tremendously abundant, as the gray partridges are in Hungary, by looking after them properly. This means, simply, to check or to reduce, as far as possible, the losses due to their natural enemies and to climate; to stop the entire destruction of the covers and the loss of natural foods; to protect the birds against fires, floods, and illegal destruction (especially during the nesting season).

I have visited many places where these matters have been attended to, and, at some of them, the birds were fully as abundant as it was desirable to have them; and they remain plentiful although thousands are shot every season. Many quail clubs quite near New York have purchased and introduced the quail on lands which they rent for this purpose and they have excellent shooting and will continue to do so until the increasing population makes it impractical to have game of any kind so near a large city. The annual dues in some of these clubs are only $10 or $15 and the sport and the food obtained are well worth the money. In many places there would be no birds, and, of course, no shooting without such industry.*

*Quail shooting is prohibited in Ohio, in New York, excepting Long Island, and is prohibited or restricted to short seasons and small bags elsewhere. These restrictions must be increased everywhere if the laws prohibit profitable quail breeding.

.

The mountain partridge, the plumed partridge, and the San Pedro partridge, the three species popularly known as California mountain quail are so much alike that they may be regarded as the same for sporting purposes. They are larger than the bob-whites and are easily distinguished by the plume of long, straight feathers. The length of the plumed partridges is about 10 inches; bob-white is about 7% inches.

I did not find these birds very abundant anywhere in my rambles in California, but Elliot says the mountain partridge is rather abundant in the Willamette Valley, Oregon and common in parts of California. The plumed partridge inhabits the drier regions of the interior and only approaches the seacoast in the southern portions of its range. The San Pedro species inhabits the San Pedro Mountains, Lower California.

The flesh of these beautiful big game birds is palatable and, although they do not perform as well before dogs as the bobwhites, they are well worth preserving as objects of sport and for food. Like other upland game birds they have vanished rapidly and they are extinct in many places. Something more than shooting them even under laws providing for short seasons and small bags is necessary to save them from extinction Game keepers easily could keep them fairly plentiful and could preserve, at the same time, the big dusky grouse, the band tailed pigeon and many California valley quails on properly protected areas. A regulated market should supply the funds to support the needed industry.

The food of the young is largely insects. Later the birds eat berries, many seeds and buds, and Elliot says they eat grain when it is obtainable. This is a useful hint for game preservers, who should always see that the game has plenty of food. The nests of the plumed and mountain partridges usually contain from eight to ten or twelve eggs.

Valley Quail or partridges and the California quail are much alike in size and markings. The valley quail is somewhat paler in color and inhabits the interior of

Oregon, Nevada and California, south to Cape St. Lucas, the California species being more a native of the coast regions. The food habits of both are similar to those of the other quails. Complaints have been made that these birds when abundant are injurious to vineyards. In addition to the seed, grains, berries, buds and insects the game preserver might well plant a lot of grapes as an additional food supply for them. No doubt they would eat raisins in winter, as pheasants and other game birds will, and condemned raisins or raisins of the cheaper grades might be used to advantage on game farms and preserves.

Although these birds are found abundant in warm climates, they also thrive in mountainous regions and they can stand a lot of cold and snow if they have plenty of food and grit and are protected from the furred and feathered enemies referred to elsewhere. They run before the dogs, but when scattered they often afford good sport. I found them tremendously abundant some years ago when from thirty to fifty covies often were observed dusting themselves in the roads in an afternoon's drive.

Gambrel's Quail is a beautiful game bird somewhat similar to the California valley quail, but it has the same fault and often relies on its legs when the sportsman would prefer to see it use its wings. The range includes parts of California and thence east through Arizona and New Mexico to western Texas. A few years ago thousands of these birds were shot for the markets and since no one protected them against the snakes, hawks, and their other numerous enemies they quickly became extinct in many places and were threatened with extinction everywhere. On some big quail ranches in Arizona and New Mexico, in charge of competent game keepers, these birds might be made and kept far more plentiful than they ever were, and such industry will pay as soon as birds from game farms can be sold for propagation and the food produced can be freely marketed. It is to be hoped that the profitable breeding of these birds will be undertaken before it is too late. These birds, like the other Western and Southwestern partridges, are runners, but they are said to afford considerable sport when they are scattered; like the others they are very good to eat. The lands they inhabit support many cacti, which afford protection from their natural enemies but which are bad for bird dogs. In addition to other enemies, including wolves and snakes, the Gila monster is said to dine on this partridge.

An Odd Game Enemy—Gila Monster

The scaled partridge and the chestnut-bellied scaled partridge are two excellent wild food birds, identical in appearance save that the last named has a chestnut patch on the belly. The birds are found in the Rio Grande Valley, Texas, and northern Mexico; the first named form is found also in New Mexico, southern Arizona and the Valley of Mexico. Like the other Western birds they are runners.

I once had a flock in my room for a time, and the speed they made when they started on a course around the room against the wall was most remarkable. I would have backed them against the fastest Gambols or Valley Quails that ever ran on a desert or prairie. The country inhabited often is full of thorns which prevent the use of dogs and render the shooting comparatively uninteresting. Natural foods undoubtedly are sufficiently plentiful in most parts of their range, since the birds once were very plentiful. The control of their enemies would seem to be all that is necessary to perpetuate the birds for sport.

MEARN'S QUAIL is an interesting bird. It is about the size of bob-white, but it is unmistakable on account of its peculiar markings. The head is black and brown, marked with white as indicated in the illustration. The upper parts are brown barred with black, the sides of the breast and flanks are almost black

25

and dotted with white, which causes the bird to look something like a dark little guinea-hen.

I have never shot this bird and, in fact, they are nowhere common, and, possibly, now are extinct in the United States, excepting the birds purchased and owned by breeders. Their flesh is excellent and I have no doubt they can be made an attractive addition to the game bag.

Our bob-white has a wide range through- out the United States from southern Canada to the Gulf states, and westward to the Great Plains. It has been introduced in Colorado, Utah and as far west as California and Oregon. In a California State report, a few years ago, it was stated that the birds first liberated disappeared, excepting in one place where they were protected from their natural enemies.*

It would not be surprising if our markets be supplied with an abundance of quail from Oregon and other Western states, since the people are enterprising and they seem to understand the value of practical game preservation.

From Massachusetts north, in New England, and in the northern parts of most of our Northern states the quail

*Mr. D. Baldwin, one of the State Game Commissioners of Montana, says in The Game Breeder's Magazine that twenty-four bob-whites were purchased in Kansas by a few sportsmen, before it was illegal to sell birds for breeding purposes, and liberated in the Ealispell valley. He estimates there must be from fifteen to twenty thousand quail in the valley.

suffers much from the severe winters and it is not so easily kept plentiful. But stock birds have been trapped in cold mountainous regions and held in barns until spring with very little trouble and with very good results, and some birds easily might be preserved for sport in all of the Northern states. The big quail preserves are, for the most part, in the Carolinas and other Southern states, where land is cheap, natural foods are abundant, and where the climate is excellent for game preserving.

A Future Covey of Quail.

On the Southern farms the birds easily are kept plentiful. A game keeper once asked me, as with good dogs we strolled over his grounds, where thousands of quail had just been shot, if I did not think he had too many birds. Undoubtedly he had and his decision to "thin them out" before the breeding season was correct. I regretted that the birds lost in the "thinning" process could not be legally marketed for either propagation or as food. Soon, however, I predict there will be many commercial game farms in the South and they surely will make a lot of money until the business is overdone.

Many experiments have been made with the artificial breeding of bob-whites. The birds lay, even in small pens, and although it is generally believed that the males and females have decided preferences in the selection of their mates, pairs have been arbitrarily mated, often, and the hens usually lay fertile eggs, and persist in laying when the eggs are stolen. Mr. Herbert Job secured over seventy eggs from one quail and the Massachusetts Commission secured over a hundred eggs from one. Several times as many eggs as are laid in a wild state can be counted on, and artificial breeding would seem to be inviting to sportsmen and to commercial game farmers. But the experiments thus far have resulted in many losses of young birds by diseases and no one has succeeded in producing large numbers of good healthy quail.

The hand-rearing of these birds is not necessary, since quickly and inexpensively they can be made to swarm on protected areas, when breeding wild, and wild bred birds are the best for sport and for food. I am inclined to predict that in America as in England and on the continent of Europe, the artificial breeding of quail only will be attempted in a comparatively few places in order to try and help out the wild breeding birds which for any reason do not seem to thrive.

The quail is fond of farming regions, especially where wheat and the other small grains are cultivated. It thrives in the South on cow-peas and many other foods which are plentiful. It is quite as important to see that the foods the birds require at different seasons of the year are plentiful and that they have proper covers and protection, as it is to see that the enemies are controlled. Good shooting depends on a proper attention being given to all of these matters.

Briars, both berry and flower briars, the blackberry, the wild rose and many others, make safe and attractive covers and they also furnish much food. The young quails live largely on insects found in the fields and woods. Later they eat many berries and the seeds of plants, including weeds. In the fall they glean the stubbles for the grain lost at the
harvest and in winter they often live on sumac, wild rose hips and other plants which are seen above the snow. At this season many birds will perish unless food be supplied. A little corn, served with grit, at various established feeding places will save hundreds of birds during a severe winter. Mr. H. J. Montanus, of the Middle Island Club, near New York, informed me last winter that their quail were feeding regularly at many established feeding places, at some of which several covies came to dine together.

"JUGGING"

WE have four splendid grouse of the open country which formerly were tremendously abundant. The prairie grouse, the sharp-tailed grouse, the heath-hen, and the su.ge grouse comprise the best group of grouse to be found anywhere in the world. They all lie well to the dogs and are excellent food birds. The former abundance of these birds is almost beyond belief. Tons of them once were shipped to the Eastern markets at a single consignment. I have shot on the Western prairies when it was an easy matter to bag a wagon load of grouse in a half-day's shooting by two guns. The birds now are extinct in entire states and never can be restored excepting by private industry, since it is absolutely necessary to preserve some of the wild grasses, roses, sunflowers, and other covers which will not be preserved in closely cultivated regions unless it pays to do so.

In the states where the grouse still occur most of the farms are posted against all shooting and many of the states now prohibit grouse shooting absolutely. But the birds must continue to vanish in places where their natural covers and foods are destroyed, because they become an easy prey to their over-abundant natural enemies and they must perish in the winter, when none of the natural foods remain in sight above the snow. No birds need more immediate attention from the sportsmen; no group of birds is more valuable from an economic point of view than the grouse of the open country. In many of the grouse states the state game officers are introducing foreign game birds in large numbers and they seem to be aware that the grouse cannot be preserved on closely cultivated farms as objects of public pursuit. Some intelligent state game officers, I am pleased to observe, are prepared to urge breeders' enactments making it worthwhile to save these birds, and I recently had a letter from a Western officer in which he said he would favor the needed industry and would be glad to see syndicates of sportsmen formed to save the grouse.

As the matter now stands the shooting practically has ended and most naturalists predict the extermination of these birds. The country is so big (hundreds of times as big as the grouse lands of the old world) that there is room enough for all American sportsmen to have good grouse shooting for all time to come, provided we undertake the practical preservation of our grouse before it is too late.

The birds are being protected in some places, but it is evident that only a few persons can be expected to engage in the needed industry so long as the shooting and the sale of the game is prohibited. Grouse multiply rapidly when the covers and foods are preserved and their enemies are controlled and they can be made more abundant than they ever were.

Some Grouse of the Open Country.

The sharp-tailed or pin-tailed grouse is very similar in size and weight to its cousin the prairie grouse. It is lighter in color and more gray, and has a short pointed tail which suggested the name. I have had many good days shooting these birds on the Northwestern plains when they were abundant. They lie well to the dog and fly a mile or more alternately whirring and sailing on extended wings so that it is desirable to shoot them from a wagon or on horseback.

The range of the sharp-tailed grouse is from Canada and Michigan to New Mexico and westward to parts of California, and to Alaska. It is said to be still fairly abundant in some parts of Oregon and Washington but it has been reported as extinct or mF nearly so in California and in other parts of its range. Its food is similar to that of the prairie grouse. Many grasshoppers and other insects are eaten, the young being highly insectivorous like all the other grouse, the quails, and the turkeys. The vegetable food comprises leaves, buds and flowers; weed seeds, fruit, and grain. Since this is the more northern species, it naturally relies more on buds than the prairie grouse does, and in winter it eats birch buds, willow buds, and others. I have seen this bird alight on trees more often than the prairie grouse does, but it lies equally well to the dogs, does not fly to the trees when flushed, and I am inclined to regard it as the best grouse in America and I doubt if a better bird can be found in the world. Certainly it is well worth preserving and I believe it will not be long before it is restored and made plentiful and profitable on many of the big wheat farms of the Northwestern and Pacific coast states. The sharp-tail is very fond of wheat, but it cannot secure the grains beneath the snow during the long winters, and it perishes because the wild roses and other winter foods have been destroyed. A handsome border to a private road, fence or path, containing wild roses and sunflowers and prairie grasses, could be made to yield a good crop of grouse, many of which might be shot on the stubbles in the autumn without any danger of extermination. Some stock birds should be left, of course, and the prairie falcon, the coyote, the snake and other enemies should not be permitted to devour them.

A Sharp-tail

The sage cock, or cock of the plains, is the second largest grouse in the world, the capercailzie of the old world being somewhat bigger. Our sage cock is peculiar in its habits and it is found in the regions where the artemesia or wild sage grows, extensively. I have shot many of these grouse from the saddle when riding across the wide plains covered as far as the eye can reach with the gray green plants of wild sage.

The food of the sage grouse consists largely of the leaves of the wild sage which late in the year impart a bitter flavor to the meat, and which caused a Western traveler to denounce it as a "quinine brute." Early in the year the young birds live largely on grasshoppers and other insects, and I have eaten them in August when they were delicious. The flesh at this season is tender and juicy and compares favorably with that of the other grouse.

Since the natural foods for these birds still are plentiful on the vast alkaline plains, it would appear that "too much shooting" must be ascribed as the reason for their threatened extinction. The well known rule that no game birds can stand both the destruction due to natural causes and shooting also, is proved everywhere and it explains, undoubtedly, our loss of the cock of the plains.

These big grouse are well worth preserving, the lands where they dwell are practically worthless and a good big sage-cock ranch or preserve would cost almost nothing and there is room enough for all. A few mounted game keepers who understand the control of the enemies of the red grouse of the moors, could protect the cock of the plains on many square miles and such industry should be encouraged if we wish to save the grouse and to perpetuate sport.

Sage Grouse Courtship

IN pattern, marking, and color, the heath-hen is identical with the prairie grouse. It was considered by the earlier ornithologists to be an Eastern form of the abundant Western species. It was plentiful, formerly, in Massachusetts, Connecticut, and the eastern parts of New York, New Jersey, Pennsylvania, and Virginia. Large numbers of heath-hens were shot on Long Island, New York, and this was one of the first birds to be protected by law in that state. It is significant that it became extinct, like the wild turkey in Ohio, at a time when shooting was prohibited.

34

The only surviving heath-hens inhabit the island of Martha's Vineyard, Massachusetts, and it is greatly to the credit of the capable Massachusetts Game Commissioners that the birds have not been permitted to become extinct . Although shooting was prohibited, the birds continued to vanish because for a time they were not protected from their over-abundant natural enemies and from cats and roving dogs which destroyed them every season. Forest fires also destroyed many nests, and in 1890 the ornithologist William Brewster ascertained that there were only about 200 heath-hens living on the island. They have since been given some special attention by a game warden and the losses due to game enemies, fires and other causes have been checked somewhat. The biro's are said to respond slowly to this protection, but their numbers are reported to he increasing. A few skilled game keepers devoting their entire attention to the protection of these birds soon would reduce the hawks and the cats and other enemies and the increase in numbers undoubtedly would be rapid because the destruction of each enemy would mean the saving of many birds.

The bird is especially desirable since it thrives on the scrub oak lands of the Eastern states and it might be restored in places where no game of any kind now occurs. At present it is of no value to sport and, of course, it no longer is eaten. Since it was formerly sufficiently abundant to sell for only a few cents in the markets, it is evident that it can be made profitably plentiful now that all meats are dear.

The foods of the heath-hen, as given by the earlier ornithologists, are the bay berry , which abounds hi many parts of Martha's Vineyard, the partridge berry, cranberry, rose hips, acorns, and pine and alder buds. There are many places where these foods are sufficiently plentiful to support a good head of heath-hens and it is to be hoped they may be restored to their former range.

Inspecting Heath Hen Country

The PRAIRIE GROUSE

The prairie grouse or "chicken," including the somewhat smaller form which is found in Texas and Louisiana, still occurs, in sadly diminished numbers, from Manitoba, Michigan, and Indiana to Texas and westward to the great plains where, as in the Dakotas, it has extended its range with the advancement of civilization. When I first went to North Dakota, to shoot the sharp-tailed grouse, the common prairie chicken was scarce, but later it increased in numbers in some parts of the state and it could be kept plentiful on most of the open ground as far west as the Rocky Mountains.

The prairie grouse weighs about two pounds and its flesh is tender, juicy, and delicious. Some prefer it to the flesh of the ruffed grouse and I am inclined to side with them. It certainly is a magnificent wild food bird and well worth preserving. The way to save it from extinction, paradoxical as it may seem, is' to keep the markets full of grouse during a long open season. The money received from the sale of some grouse will enable sportsmen of small means to meet the expenses of looking after the birds and dealing fairly with the farmers who have posted their lands.

Grouse cannot stand the ordinary destruction by natural enemies and the destruction by guns at the same time. Since the birds continued to vanish after shooting had been prohibited, it is evident that there are other causes for this besides shooting. The destruction of their foods and covers are sufficient to account for the loss. Cats, rats, and roving dogs in many places prevent any increase in their numbers. Prairie fires and floods often exterminate them on large areas. The same may be said of the sharp-tailed grouse, and the "prairie chicken" of the Northwestern states which once was plentiful as far west as California; this bird has suffered, also, from the loss of its food and covers. The prairie grasses, the wild rose, the wild sunflower and many other food plants often are absolutely destroyed on the big wheat farms where these birds formerly were abundant and where they are now extinct or nearly so. In addition to food the briars afford safe protection when a hawk or other enemy approached. I have seen a line of telegraph poles across a big wheat stubble when there appeared to be a hawk on nearly every pole, and there was absolutely no place where a grouse could hide on the vast prairie which extended to the horizon. Of course there were no grouse. I found the sharp-tailed chicken very abundant in the valley of the Rosebud, Montana, in the days when it was hardly safe to shoot there on account of the Indians, but the wild roses were also very abundant and afforded protection to the birds and food in the

37

winter, when they lived largely upon the rose hips which could be seen above the snow. If we give the natural enemies a good chance to eat them, by destroying the prairie chicken's nesting sites and covers, and if we destroy absolutely their winter foods on vast areas, we must not expect the birds to return to places where they have become extinct because we have enacted laws prohibiting shooting.

Prairie Grouse in "The Old, Old Story"

The food habits of the prairie grouse are well known. They eat many insects, especially grasshoppers, from May to October, and are valuable aids to the farmer for this reason. In the fall and winter the food of the prairie grouse is mainly vegetable; fruit, leaves flowers, shoots, seeds and grain. Dr. Judd says: "Like the bob-white and the ruffed grouse, the prairie grouse is fond of rose hips and the abundant roses of the prairie yield 11.01 per cent of its food." In Kansas and many other states the wild sunflowers, goldenrod and other natural foods were tremendously abundant, but throughout most of the range of the grouse these foods have been destroyed absolutely. It would pay to restore some prairie grass, wild roses, sunflowers and other covers and foods which are essential to the birds' existence. No farmer or sportsman can be expected to give the land, time, labor, and money needed to save the grouse simply as a bait for trespassers.

This grouse is fond of the stubble as a feeding ground and it can be made profitably abundant on many farms, but it must have winter foods and covers, and it must be protected from its enemies if any shooting is to be done; otherwise it will become extinct.

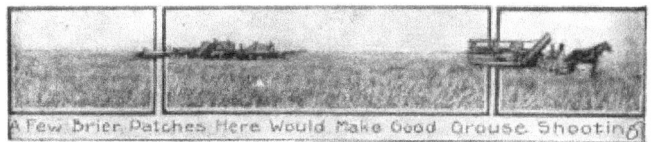

A Few Drier Patches Here Would Make Good Grouse Shooting

Dr. Judd says this grouse yields readily to domestication and says preserves for domesticated birds should be established. He relies on Audubon's statement, that "the pinnated grouse is easily tamed." The recent experiments which have come to my notice have been failures; and since the birds now are very valuable, it seems peculiar that there are no published reports of successful hand-rearing. It is certain, however, that the birds can be made very abundant as the red grouse have been on the moors of Scotland. Practically all of the grouse bred in Scotland are wild birds. Few experiments in hand-rearing have been made and they are not necessary or desirable. As I have observed, wild bred birds are the cheapest and most easily and safely reared; evidently they are better for sport and better able to take care of themselves than hand-reared birds.

Probably ninety per cent of the farms where these birds occur are now posted against shooting and the number of farms so protected is increasing. There are hundreds of thousands of square miles where the grouse shooting can be made good as it is in Scotland, provided the farmers be dealt with fairly. A grouse preserve, properly conducted, will prove to be a money-maker. Since late in the year this grouse has a well sustained flight and often will go a mile or more before alighting, the farm where any practical preserving is undertaken should be a big one, or the shooting on a number of farms should be under one management. Certainly no one will be damaged if such industry be encouraged on the farms which are now posted against all gunners or on the farms where the grouse have become extinct.

GROUSE shooting in Scotland is the grand opera of the world's shooting. Many thousands of sportsmen go to the moors every

August to shoot the red grouse. The birds are bred wild and are shot for the most part by driving, when the birds are flushed and sent over the guns. So popular are the moors that a vast throng is attracted. The president of an English railroad is reported to have said: "The grouse pay our dividends." Many sportsmen from the Continent of Europe and many Americans go to Scotland on the 12th of August, when the season opens, and one season an English magazine stated that an American sportsman had the best dogs on the moors. Complaints have been heard about our countrymen because they are said to have raised the prices of the shooting rentals and to have taken some of the more desirable places from Englishmen who formerly rented them from year to year. Tons of grouse are shipped to the English markets; many thousands of these birds are sold and eaten in America; but the shooting remains good. There is no fear of extermination.

The ornithologist, Elliot, in concluding his chapter on the American prairie grouse, which, as a sporting and food bird, is very similar to the red grouse of Scotland, says: "But the inevitable day will surely come that will bring the same fate to all our wild creatures, and the prairie chicken, like other natives of the wilderness, will remain only as a memory."

We should take notice that "the inevitable day" is almost here. The size of the impending catastrophe becomes evident when we observe that the area of Scotland which supplies the English markets with cheap grouse is only 30,405 square miles. Since there are some grouse in Northern England and parts of Ireland, it would be fair to say that the food producing area is about 50,000 square miles. The combined area of the states where our grouse of the open country still occur (in sadly diminished numbers) may be roughly estimated as 2,350,000 square miles. We have besides about 230,000 square miles in the states where the prairie grouse have become extinct, and in one of these states, Audubon says, they were so abundant as to be regarded as pests. They can be restored and made plentiful for sport and for a highly desirable food supply, provided the matter is attended to now.

Grouse shooting has been prohibited in many states, and in no state can these birds be sold as food. It is evident, therefore, that it does not pay to look after them properly; to restore the prairie grass for nesting sites and cover, and to preserve the wild roses, sunflowers and other plants, which furnish protection and food and which have been destroyed throughout the range of the grouse in the interest of agriculture. If only a small portion of the area suitable for grouse breeding be utilized for the profitable production of these birds they might be made more abundant than they ever were and all of the sportsmen in America and many from abroad might have shooting sufficiently good to feed the people with cheap grouse. All that is needed is a little encouragement for those who are willing to undertake the needed industry.

39

THE cost of breeding game in a wild state is small when compared with the cost of hand-rearing pheasants and other game bred in captivity. The wild nesting birds find most of their food in the fields. The grouse, like the quail, glean the stubbles after the harvest and they can subsist in large numbers, even in severe winters, on the hips of the wild rose and the seeds of sunflowers, sumacs and other plants. The farmers, whose farms are posted, often are quite willing to rent the shooting for a few cents per acre, and if skilled game keepers be employed to control the natural enemies of the birds and to see that they have proper nesting sites and foods the grouse can quickly be made profitable, and syndicates of sportsmen formed to share the expense of looking after them can have splendid shooting at very small cost. As I have observed, the sportsmen who are looking after the quail often pay only $10 to $15 each per year, and if they could sell some of their quail these amounts would be reduced.

Since it is very evident that as population increases the grouse shooting must be prohibited everywhere unless the birds are properly looked after, I sincerely hope it will not be long before grouse shooting is restored on many of the posted farms, from Louisiana and Texas to Michigan and North Dakota, by syndicates of sportsmen who are willing to deal fairly with the owners of the grouse lands and to persuade them to assist in making these splendid birds profitably plentiful as the red grouse are in Scotland. We should always remember that most of the farms are now posted against all shooting and that the farmers are supplementing this prohibition with laws prohibiting the taking of grouse at any time. There are good reasons why these conditions must remain and grow worse unless the grouse be preserved, in the interest of sport, on at least a part of the vast area they should inhabit.

THE grouse of the woods and mountains which inhabit the American woods and mountains are the well-known ruffed grouse the Canada grouse or spruce partridge, the dusky or blue grouse of the Rocky Mountain region and the ptarmigans which live above the timber line of the Rocky Mountains within the United States and thence north to the arctic tundra of Alaska. They are all excellent sporting birds, highly prized as food and well worth preserving.

The ptarmigans are circumpolar and always are plentiful in foreign markets.

They no longer occur on vast mountain areas where formerly they were plentiful in the United States, and throughout their range they have diminished in numbers where shooting is permitted, for the very good reason that no species can withstand this additional check to its <_ increase unless it be properly looked after and protected J^ from its natural enemies.

SOMEWHAT smaller and darker than the ruffed grouse, the Canada or spruce grouse is by no means so good as our woodland drummer, either for sport or on the table. The two forms or species, which are much alike, inhabit the northern coniferous forests from northern Maine to Oregon and Washington. The Western form, termed Franklin's grouse, is much like its relative which is found east of the Rocky Mountains.

Ptarmigan

The spruce grouse are more plentiful in Canada and Alaska than they are in the United States. They are familiar to big game hunters and often they are shot for food, but they are too tame in most wood lands to afford good sport, and they appear so stupid that they are called "fool hens" by residents of the Western mountains. Many have been taken by a noose fastened to the end of a fishing rod or stick, the noose being dropped over the head of the unsuspicious birds which are then easily jerked off the branch of the tree. Elliot says he has seen birds push the noose aside with their bills when it touched their heads without slipping over.

The spruce grouse frequents tamarack swamps and woods where the spruce and fir grow thickest; the leaves, buds and tender shoots of the coniferous trees make up a good part of their food. Like the ruffed grouse and the dusky grouse, these birds eat many berries and other fruits in the summer; bearberries, blueberries, juniper berries, bunch berries and the wax currant berry are the principal berries eaten. At this season the flesh is palatable, but later in the year and in winter when the food consists largely of the spruce shoots, which suggested the name of the bird, the flesh becomes bitter and undesirable.

The nest contains usually from ten to twelve eggs, sometimes as many as sixteen. It is placed on the ground, and only one

brood is hatched in a season

BLUE or dusky grouse are from four to six inches longer than the average ruffed grouse. The blue grouse weighs from 2½ to 3½ pounds; the weight of the ruffed grouse is 2 pounds and often less. The range of the three ornithological forms of the blue grouse (which from the sportsman's viewpoint may be considered as one species, since the appearance and habits are much like is from Alaska to New Mexico and Arizona. The Western form inhabits the coast range from California and it occurs eastward to Nevada, western Idaho and thence to northern Alaska. I have observed these birds when they were abundant in the Rocky Mountains and so tame as to share the name "fool hen." Like the other grouse, it is disappearing so rapidly everywhere and has become extinct in so many places that laws prohibiting grouse shooting at all times have been deemed necessary. In many places the birds remaining are wild enough for sport, and they lie well to the dog.

Canada Grouse

The blue grouse are mountain as well as forest loving birds, and they often wander from the spruce and fir forests above the timber line in their search for berries and other food. In winter they descend to the valleys. They are not migratory, such movements being made solely in search of food and to escape the severe weather of the higher altitudes.

The food of the blue grouse consists of insects, which form a large part of the food of the young birds, grasshoppers being the principal insect eaten, and fruit, seeds and leaves. Like the spruce grouse, the blue grouse is a browser and is one of our chief foliage-eating birds. Dr. Judd says it spends most of its time in pine forests feeding on needles, buds and flowers. In the summer many berries are eaten, among them the abundant wild gooseberries, currants, strawberries, huckleberries, service and bear-berries. The flesh is white, tender, juicy and delicious. Later in the season it is affected by the change in diet and it often has then a bitter and resinous taste which renders it highly undesirable. Like the other grouse, the dusky grouse nests on the ground in May or June. Usually there are about eight eggs, sometimes more. The birds should be shot in September and October, when they are desirable for the table, and if properly looked after on some good-sized preserves the markets can be kept full of them without decreasing their numbers from year to year.

The enemies of these grouse are eagles as well as hawks, and mountain lions, lynx and other species of ground vermin, including snakes.

OUR woodland drummer, the ruffed grouse, has been properly named the king of game birds. It is the best woodland grouse in the world, and it should always be as plentiful in our markets as the European black-cock is, not only in foreign markets, but also in New York. The practical and profitable preservation of the ruffed grouse on comparatively small areas would result in their remaining plentiful throughout the surrounding country. The shooting can be made good on thousands of square miles where the birds now are few in number or entirely extinct. Where they are properly looked after they will thrive even in small woodlands and bushy tracts, provided they contain the foods they require and their enemies be controlled.

Many experiments have been made in the artificial propagation of this species, with some success. Professor Hodge hand-reared a number of birds in his yard at Worcester, Massachusetts, and the Massachusetts game department and others have reared a few birds. I do not, however, regard the artificial rearing of grouse as necessary or even desirable. The losses often are large, and, for sporting purposes as well as for food, birds reared in a wild state in protected woods are the best and by far the cheapest; they can be made as abundant as it is desirable to have them.

Many believe that the ruffed grouse wanders over a wide territory and that it would be difficult to breed them in small woods. They undoubtedly wander long distances in search of food. Young birds hatched in a locality where insects are plentiful and where there is an abundance of mast for the old birds will be led away later to places where berries are plentiful, for this grouse is a great berry-eater.

Since game preserving has become popular in America and the necessity for it has become well-known, more attention has been given to the food habits and other requirements of all our game birds than was formerly given to this subject. Proper covers also are important. This bird's existence depends on them, since the entire destruction of forests will result in the extermination of woodland species. But the ruffed grouse can be kept plentiful even in closely settled farming regions, provided small woods or thickets be. left or are planted, and foods suitable for different seasons of the year are kept plentiful. Young birds are largely insectivorous. More than ninety-five per cent of the diet of the young grouse examined by Dr. Judd was insects. Newly hatched chicks eat the most; as they grow older they eat fruit, and later they feed on mast, grain and buds. The study of the food habits of the young has not been as extensive as it should be, but indicates that the chicks eat grasshoppers, cutworms, certain beetles, ants, parasitic wasps, buffalo tree hoppers, spiders, grubs and caterpillars.

Undoubtedly many small insects and their eggs which are found in the woods and adjacent fields will be added to the list. The beetles seem to be preferred, but Dr. Judd says the grouse he shot in September, in New Hampshire, were feeding largely on red-legged grasshoppers, which were abundant in the pastures where the birds foraged. The vegetable food consists largely of seeds, fruit, buds and leaves. Mast, including hazelnuts, beechnuts, chestnuts and acorns are staple foods, the acorns being the largest supply in many regions. Acorns of the scrub oak, scrub chestnut oak, white oak and red oak are swallowed whole, and I have often found the grouse abundant in the scrub oaks on Long Island, New York, and in other regions where there were few or no large trees. The ruffed grouse undoubtedly eats grain and often procures it along woodland roads, where it resorts to dust, and to feed on the abundant berries.

More than one-fourth of the yearly food of this bird is fruit. Its diet includes the hips of the wild rose, grapes, partridge berries, thorn apples, wild crab apples, cultivated apples, winter- green berries, bayberries, blueberries, huckleberries black-berries, raspberries, strawberries, cranberries, sarsaparilla berries, and others; wild and cultivated cherries, plums, haws, sumacs, including the poison sumac and poison ivy, which are taken with immunity.

Sportsmen are well aware of the fondness of this grouse for wild grapes and apples, and they often find them in places where grapes are plentiful and in old fruit orchards, especially on abandoned farms. The wild rose hips and sumacs are excellent winter foods because they can be obtained above the snow. Wild and cultivated sunflowers furnish excellent food, and many other fruits and seeds of varying importance are on the ruffed grouse's bill of fare.

Birch, poplar, willow, laurel and other buds are eaten by the ruffed grouse, and the budding, practiced for the most part during the winter, enables it to survive the severe winters of the Northern states and Canada, when other foods are buried in deep snows. The several species of birch buds are a staple.

There is no better bird on the table than a ruffed grouse shot in September or October, excepting, possibly, the prairie grouse and sharp-tailed grouse. Its diet at this season is largely made up of fruits and beechnuts, chestnuts, acorns, etc., audit is not surprising that the flesh of the well-bred grouse is pronounced delicious by all epicures.

The ruffed grouse has numerous enemies which must be controlled if any shooting is to be done. Certain hawks, owls and crows are the chief feathered enemies; the goshawk is often called the partridge hawk on account of its fondness for ruffed grouse. The great horned owl and the barred owl take many grouse which escape the fox at night roosting in the trees.
Foxes, weasels, minks, skunks and other furry enemies are fond of grouse. Snakes destroy both birds and eggs. The combined toll taken in a year by these enemies is large, and when the enemies are controlled it is evident the grouse supply must be big enough to stand a lot of shooting. Roving dogs and cats, both wild and domestic, do much damage in the grouse woods and should be exterminated. Forest fires at the nesting season are especially destructive, but these also will be controlled when it pays to preserve the birds properly.

Ruffed grouse prefer deciduous trees to evergreens. A forest of mast and fruit-bearing trees, with some evergreens, is far better for grouse than an evergreen forest with few deciduous trees. The grouse nests on the ground usually against a fallen log, stump, tree or other obstruction which may protect it from a rear attack and will often cause its enemy to pass to either side without discovering the nest. This usually contains from 8 to 12 eggs, and sometimes more.

More than Just a Game Enemy

It is only a few years since the breeding of wild ducks for sport and for profit was undertaken in England. Everyone thought that to attempt wild duck breeding simply would result in providing sport for others than those who reared the ducks, because they are migratory. Some experiments, however, made with mallards, by game keepers, were very successful and it was ascertained that if the ducks are properly fed, and if they are not shot on or about the breeding ponds, they will remain to furnish good shooting and that they will attract many migrating birds to the feeding grounds and waters. It was not long before nearly every country place in England had wild ducks, and many shooting clubs, or syndicates, as they say in England, were formed by sportsmen to share the expenses of duck breeding.

The wild ducks are more easily reared than pheasants. The breeding ducks are kept about a small pond in a yard or field wired against vermin with a fence of chicken wire. The ducks lay their eggs in little brush covers which are provided for them. If the eggs are gathered daily they persist in laying, and on an average about thirty eggs can be obtained from each duck.

When the waters are small it is best to have one drake for every two or three ducks, but on large waters it is better to increase the number of drakes. The young ducks when one day old are taken to a grassy rearing field where the hen is confined in a coop, as in pheasant rearing, and the young ducks are permitted to chase insects in the grass. Many breeders advise not letting the young go to the water until they are eight or nine weeks old, and many ducks are reared by this method. It is important that the young birds should have plenty of water to drink, which is furnished in little pans placed in front of the coops.

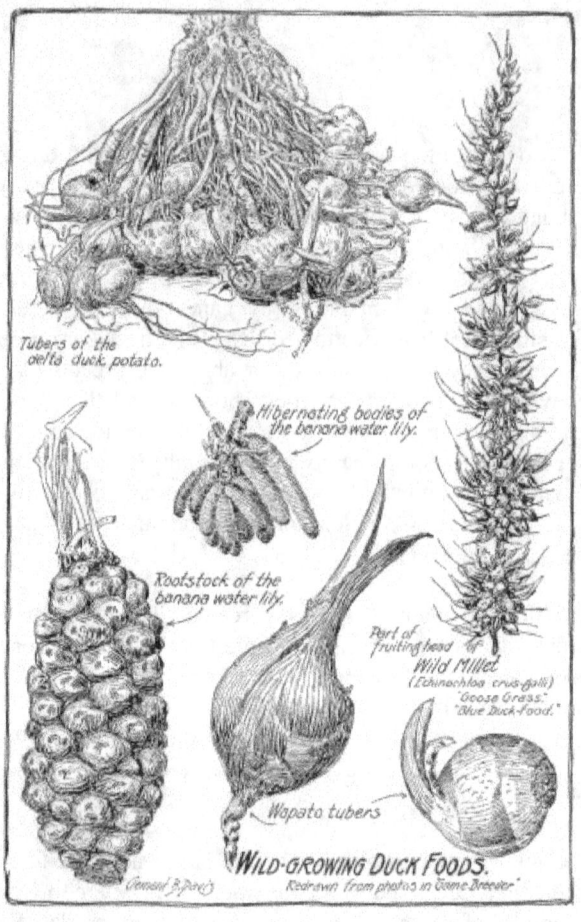

Tubers of the delta duck potato.

Hibernating bodies of the banana water lily.

Rootstock of the banana water lily.

Part of fruiting head of Wild Millet
(Echinochloa crus-galli)
"Goose Grass."
"Blue Duck-food."

Wapato tubers

WILD-GROWING DUCK FOODS.

Redrawn from photos in "Game Breeder"

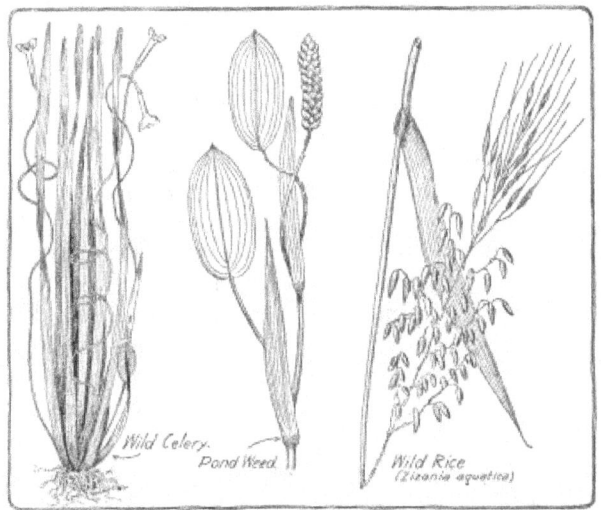

Wild Celery.
Pond Weed.
Wild Rice
(Zizania aquatica)

It is of the utmost importance that ducklings have plenty of shade, since they are affected by a complaint called "straddies" when permitted to run in fields where no shade is provided. The complaint is easily detected : the young ducks appear to be dizzy and soon fall and expire. It is said to be similar to sunstroke. I have seen hundreds of ducks die in this manner on a hot, sandy field, even when shade was provided, and last year at The Game Breeders' Association preserve we took all of the ducks, when a day or two old, to the side of a shallow pond and placed the hens in their coops on the bank, letting the little ducks swim in the shallow water. The result was excellent. We had no trouble whatever from "sunstroke" nor in fact, from any cause. The pond where the ducks were liberated was wired with chicken wire a few feet from the shore to keep out turtles, big fish and frogs, all of which kill and eat young ducks, and the coops also were protected by a wire fence to keep out foxes, skunks and other ground enemies. Traps were placed on tall poles and in trees and many hawks and great horned owls which took some ducks were trapped and prevented from doing much damage.

The water was warm and shallow and the weather remained positively hot. Abundant shade was provided about the coops. The ducklings when in charge of hens are inclined to stay in the water too long and they often suffer from cramps, and large numbers die when the water and the weather are cold. It is for this reason many duck breeders do not permit the young birds to go near the water until they are old enough to be safely turned out on the ponds. The duck mother will lead her young brood out on the bank after a short swim and will warm them by collecting them under her wings and body on a sunny bank. I have often seen them do this, but the hen, of course, does not go into the water, and she cannot lead the young birds out at the proper time. My experiments lead me to believe that in hot weather, especially when the ducks are hatched late, it is safer to take them to a warm shallow water than it is to attempt to rear them in a very hot field. At the first drop in the thermometer the birds should be removed from the water and a wire should be run between it and the coops to prevent their going to it and catching the cramps. Cold rains with hail are bad for young ducks and they should be shut up during storms. If these matters are properly attended to the rearing of ducks will be found quite easy, since they are almost free from diseases and grow rapidly. After they are well feathered there should be no appreciable losses, provided the natural enemies be well controlled and provided the natural foods they secure about the pond be supplemented daily with a meal or two of cracked corn, and later whole corn.

1 Canvas-back Duck.
2 Scaup Duck.
3 Wood Duck.

The young ducks are fed for the first few weeks with a special wild duck meal, which is supplied by the dealers in game foods. When they procure many water-insects, bugs, worms, small frogs and fish, they will not require to be fed more than two or three times a day, and it always is desirable not to feed either young ducks or pheasants too much. See that they are eating all that is given to them, and that no food remains after a meal to become stale and unwholesome. Modern breeders keep their birds a little hungry and they get more exercise on that account in their search for natural foods.

The ducks which lend themselves most readily to hand- rearing are the mallards, from which are descended our common green-headed ducks of the barn yard, and the black ducks, often popularly termed black mallards. These birds cross readily and there are many ducks sold as black ducks which have a visible admixture of mallard, but which is so slight sometimes as to make it difficult for experts to be sure that the birds are not thoroughbred.

Since pheasants have interbred and the hybrids are desirable from the sporting viewpoint, there should not be much objection to black ducks even with a visible admixture of mallard, provided the cross is from a wild and not a barn-yard strain. The strong flight which sport demands will not be produced often by barn-yard ducks. Pure bred birds, of course, are desirable, and where only one species is reared it should be an easy matter to keep the strain pure. The mallards are more easy to hand-rear, and they breed better in captivity than the black ducks and the mallard cross is, therefore, considered desirable by some breeders.

In England the pin-tails and the English teal, a bird somewhat similar to but larger than our green-winged teal, are reared with some success on preserves and game farms. In America the wood-duck has been found easy to handle by those who understand the bird's habit of nesting in holes in trees. These birds also have been exported and many have been bred abroad, so that we now get many of our wood-ducks from Belgium and other countries where they did not occur until we furnished the stock, a sad commentary on our intelligence.

In some states the game breeders' laws only permit the profitable breeding of mallards and black ducks. This, of course, is quite absurd, since we should encourage the breeding of wood ducks and other species which most need the attention of breeders, and we should not be obliged to send money abroad to purchase American ducks. Some states encourage the profitable breeding of all game, and no doubt all of them will before long, since the game breeders' laws are popular in the states where they have been given a trial, and they have resulted in the production of a big number of wild ducks, pheasants and other game.

The sea-ducks, or deep water ducks, canvas-backs, red-heads, scaups and others, are splendid food birds, and no doubt the breeding of these fowls for sport will be attempted later. Some experiments, in fact, are now being made. I would strongly advise the breeding of these birds in a semi-wild state about the ponds and sloughs where they formerly bred in great abundance, since the easiest way always is the best way, and it is easier to breed birds in places which they have selected than it is to introduce them to places which may not seem desirable to them. The former breeding range of the canvas-back certainly extended into Michigan and Wisconsin. I have seen these birds and the other deep water ducks breeding abundantly in the Dakotas. The Black-Hawk Club, in Wisconsin, and the other duck clubs of the Northwestern states should experiment with the sea ducks and, of course, these birds can be handled on many marshes in Canada, provided the industry of duck breeding be encouraged before all of the desirable breeding grounds are drained in the interest of agriculture. I have long favored the saving of some of the duck breeding grounds. They will be saved when it is known that wild duck breeding can be made more profitable than agriculture. The Canadian marshes could supply the world with wild ducks and eggs, provided the industry were properly regulated.

A Duckling's Enemy

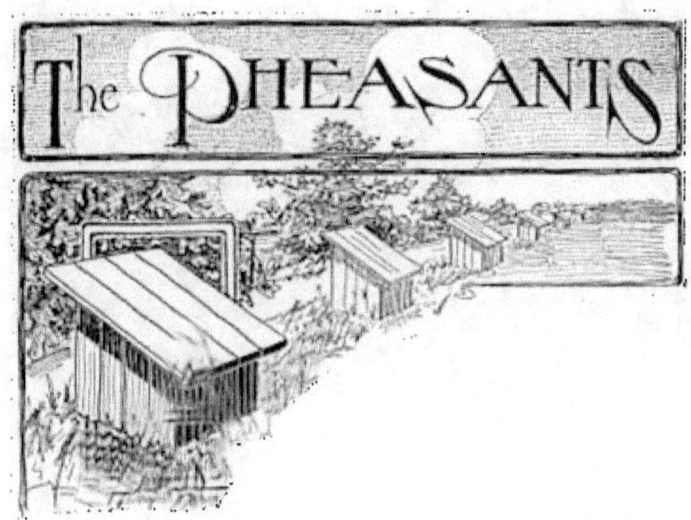

Although pheasants were introduced in England centuries ago (the date is uncertain) and their propagation has been carried on extensively by commercial game farms as well as by sportsmen, and although there was not a pheasant in America until the year 1881, when a few birds were sent from China to Oregon by Judge Denny, I firmly believe that in five or ten years, at most, there will be more pheasants in the United States than there are in any country in the world.

Partridges and the migratory quail of Europe have also been introduced in the United States and Canada in considerable numbers, but the last named vanished absolutely and experiments with this bird have been abandoned. A few capercailzie, black-cock and other birds have been imported, but only in small numbers, and the experiments with these birds are unimportant.

A foolish idea had prevailed that the foreign birds are better than our own because of their abundance abroad,
but the truth of the matter is, our grouse partridges or quails and

turkeys are by far the best game birds in the world, and if properly handled they can be kept as abundant and as cheap as the foreign birds are.

The pheasants which have been introduced have multiplied rapidly and it has been proven that they will thrive almost anywhere in the United States and in Canada, provided they be properly protected. They disappeared as "state" birds from Kansas, Ohio and other states because they cannot stand our vermin and some illegal shooting, even when shooting is prohibited.

We now have several thousand pheasant breeders, some of whom produce thousands of pheasants every year for sport. Many State Game Departments have game farms, where thousands of pheasants are reared every season, and thousands of birds are imported annually for propagation. The industry of pheasant breeding is interesting and profitable, and no good reason can be assigned why the pheasant clubs should not have pheasant-shooting, just as trap-shooting clubs have clay-bird shooting. Many now prefer to shoot something which is good to eat, and there can be no doubt the pheasant is one of the most excellent food-birds in the world.

It is absurd to say that pheasants purchased or bred by syndicates of sportsmen or by commercial game breeders belong to the state, and, under the game breeders' laws which are popular in many states, the private ownership of pheasants is recognized so long as the birds do not wander from the grounds where they are propagated by private industry. There are several hundred small breeders in Massachusetts and in a recent report issued by the Commissioners of Fisheries and Game of that state, we are told that the abundance of pheasants must depend on the many small breeders, because there are more people who can breed a few pheasants than there are who can breed thousands. In several states complaints have been made to the Agricultural Departments by farmers about the damage done by state pheasants, and in answer to an inquiry addressed by the Agricultural Department of Massachusetts, asking that if the state owned the pheasants would it remove them from the farms where they were found to be injurious, the Game Department replied that the pheasants were more beneficial than harmful and that it would not be long before they were regarded as a profitable farm crop.

In New York a county grange is reported to have asked the State Game Department to keep its pheasants out of the county. It is evident that the farmers own most of the shooting grounds and that the birds can be produced to the best advantage by those who deal fairly with the land owners as many sportsmen do. The state birds, of course, can be liberated on public lands and wild lands where the shooting is open to the public. The "overflow" from game farms and clubs adds materially to the public shooting. Many pheasants were shot for miles about the farms of The Clove Valley Club, The Game Breeders' Association, and other game breeding clubs, by persons who had never shot a pheasant until the clubs began liberating them.

The pheasant first introduced into England, which is now often called the English pheasant, is the dark-necked species, Colckicus, which has no white ring or collar about the neck. The ring-necked pheasant, Torquatus, and other species were introduced in England during the present century and the birds have interbred to such an extent that it is said to be unusual to see a pure bred dark-necked pheasant in the English markets.

The birds first introduced into the United States were the ring-necks, and these are more common everywhere than the dark-necked birds are. In Austria and Hungary many dark- necked birds are bred in a wild state and many breeders believe that this species is less likely to stray and on this account it is the better bird for wild breeding operations. I have reared many birds of both species and they seem to be equally good for hand-rearing operations. Both are good marks, but they do not lie to the dogs as well as many species of our indigenous game birds' do, excepting on certain grounds where the running is not good by reason of natural obstructions such as occur in tufted marsh fields and other places where there are barriers to speeding.

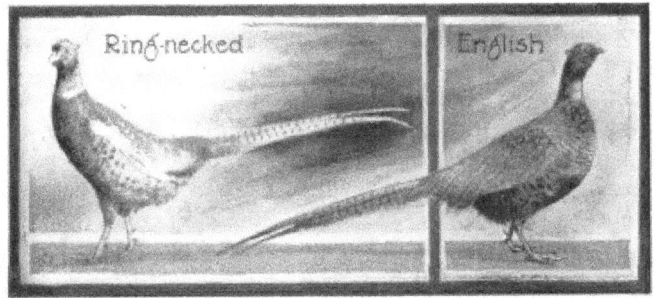

The Mongolian pheasant, a large species having the white collar, and the Prince of Wales pheasant, and a few others, are considered desirable by breeders, but the common ring-necked and dark-necked birds will, no doubt, become the most plentiful here as elsewhere.

The pheasants persist in laying when their eggs are stolen, and by hatching the eggs under barn-yard fowls it is an easy matter to have a big lot of pheasants on suitable ground. The birds thrive better on valley farms, where there are good fields of grain and grass, than they do in the mountains, where the young birds often are decimated by cold rains and where the older birds are more given to straying to seek more agreeable surroundings. The dealers in pheasant foods issue small booklets telling how to rear the birds, and while skilled game keepers, no doubt, produce the most birds, many small breeders who understand poultry have been very successful. I recently have heard from some small breeders who have been very successful. One says he sold three thousand eggs this year and had orders for several thousand more which he could not fill. The eggs sell for $25 and $30 per hundred. The live birds sell for from 85 to $7 per pair. Many birds were sold as food last season in the New York markets for $2.50 each.

The methods of hand-rearing pheasants are very similar to the methods of poultry rearers. Some breeders confine the stock birds in large pens which contain a hundred or more hens and about twenty cock birds. Little brush covers are provided and the eggs are gathered daily and hatched under barn-yard hens. Other breeders use many small pens each containing five or six hens and one cock.

When the young pheasants are one day old they are taken with their foster mothers to a rearing field where the hens are confined in coops and the chicks are permitted to run out in little yards or runs enclosed by boards or wire until they are a week or ten days old, when the fenders are removed and the little birds are permitted to have a wider range and to chase grasshoppers and other insects in the field which is enclosed with chicken wire to keep out vermin. Traps are placed on poles set in and about the field and the keeper shoots any hawks, crows or other vermin which may endeavor to take his birds.

Some breeders have permitted the hens to rim with the young birds in protected fields and woods, just as hens are permitted to move about with their chickens, and much success has resulted from this method both at State Game Farms and on private preserves.

The incubator is often used until the eggs are nearly hatched, when they are removed and placed under ordinary barn-yard hens or bantams, and later taken with the hens to the rearing field or permitted to run with the hens as above described. I had great success with some pheasants which I permitted to run in a corn field, and my friend, Mr. Bigelow, reared a lot of pheasants in this way, letting the young birds run in asparagus and rye fields. The young birds are shut up in coops at night and liberated in the morning. For the first few weeks they are fed on specially prepared meals, which are supplied by dealers with instructions for their use. Hard boiled eggs are chopped fine and mixed with the meal. Lettuce and other green foods should be supplied, also, and little pans of water should be placed in front of the coops.

I have had some good sport shooting pheasants over dogs, but in countries where they are abundant the shooting is far more difficult, because the birds are driven over the guns and they go high and fast when they are well handled. We have plenty of room for everyone who wishes to do so to have pheasants in abundance and to shoot them over dogs or by driving, as they may prefer. Pheasant clubs can be conducted with small dues, especially if other game is reared on the same grounds. I am quite sure that we soon will have an abundance of cheap pheasants in our markets, and I hope more attention will be given in the future to our quail, grouse, wild fowl and waders, which are even more interesting objects of pursuit, and equally as good, or better, as food than the pheasants.

Weasels in Winter

THE GRAY PARTRIDGE

The European gray partridge (often called Hungarian partridge) is a fine, big, brown bird somewhat larger than our quail or partridge, but it is no better on the table and by no means so good a bird in the field as our bob-white. I have had comparatively little experience with these birds. My only experiment consisted in the liberation of about a hundred on land which undoubtedly did not suit them. It was an especially dangerous place because thousands of pheasants and wild ducks were reared under wire on the adjacent land and many foxes and other predaceous animals, which were attracted to the place, found it easier to chase gray partridges than it was to get at the birds in the enclosures. The result was all the partridges were destroyed or left the place, and I became convinced that fields near those where hand-reared birds are confined are not as safe or desirable, for either quail, grouse or partridges, as fields which are not so attractive to vermin.

A few partridges were shot in the Fall several miles east of the place where my birds were liberated, but the following season local gunners told me they were extinct. The grounds were well shot over for miles about by quail shooters with excellent dogs and no partridges were observed anywhere.

I have no doubt the State Game Departments and clubs and individuals may successfully introduce these excellent game birds, but I feel sure that beat keepers must be employed before any good results will be obtained. The State Game Warden of Ohio is making an experiment this year on the lines suggested and he has sent me an excellent photograph showing a partridge nest which was taken in an unprotected field. Birds have nested, at widely separated points in other states and they have reared broods without practical protection, but later reports often indicated that none of the birds could be found. It is to be hoped that the State Departments will continue their experiments, using large numbers of partridges, and that individuals also will continue their efforts until we thoroughly understand how to make these birds plentiful. But I sincerely hope our quail and other game birds will not be neglected under the mistaken idea that they are not so good as the imported birds. Quail and grouse and their eggs have been hard to get, but the laws encouraging game breeding promise soon to remedy this unfortunate situation.

I believe it will not be long before every one who shoots will have excellent shooting both at pheasants and partridges, and also at our grouse, quail and other game, and I base the opinion upon the size of the country and the number of posted farms which can be restored to sport, and also on the rapidity with which propagation is being undertaken and the encouragement which is being given to such industry by the game breeders' enactments.

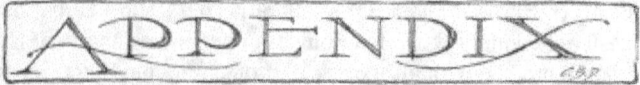

Twelve Gauge Loads Suggested for Field Shooting

It is not possible to make positive recommendation as to the best loads for shooting different kinds of game, because there are no general rules that apply under all conditions. A load that is very effective in most guns may be less so in some particular gun. In cold regions, birds are usually more heavily feathered than in warm climates and consequently it takes heavier loads to kill them. The following table represents the average for 12 ga. guns, but it may prove advisable to modify it under varying circumstances. The table of comparative loads on the next page affords a basis for determining the proper charges for different gauges.

GAME	POWDER		SHOT	
	Infallible	E. C. or Orange Extra	Quantity	Size
Rabbit............... Squirrel...............	24 grains	3 drams	1⅛ oz.	6 or 7
Quail............... Bob-White...............	24 grains	3 drams	1⅛ oz.	8 or 9
Woodcock...............	22 or 24 grains	2¾ or 3 drams	1 or 1⅛ oz.	9 or 10
Snipe............... Plover...............	24 grains	3 drams	1⅛ oz.	8 or 9
Ruffed Grouse, Pheasant or Partridge...............	24 or 25 grains	3 or 3⅛ drams	1⅛ or 1¼ oz.	6 or 7
Ducks...............	26 or 28 grains	3¼ or 3½ drams	1¼ oz.	4, 5 or 6
Geese...............	28 grains	3½ drams	1¼ oz.	1, 2 or 3
Swan............... Turkey...............	28 grains	3½ drams	1¼ oz.	T or 1
Prairie Chicken............ Pinnated Grouse............	24 or 25 grains	3 or 3⅛ drams	1⅛ or 1¼ oz.	6 or 7

Game Farming   Hercules Powder Co.

Other Antiquarian titles you may enjoy from
Hand Thrown Books

ALL ABOUT TROUT FISHING
J. A. Riddell - 1909

"As an angler who has spent most of twenty five seasons by the riverside my aim is to convey to the reader, in simple language, the outcome of actual experience, in the hope that beginners, and also more experienced anglers, may find some information that will enlighten and assist them in attaining better piscatorial results."

AMERICAN PARTRIDGE AND
PHEASANT SHOOTING – 1877 – Frank Schley

Wherein the methods of hunting partridge, quail and ruffed grouse, tips on guns and dogs and the art of wing shooting are described. "Successful shooting is the ability to measure at a glance, 30 to 50 yards with certainty. Unless you learn to judge distances accurately when in the field, you will never become certain of stopping your birds."

CULTURE OF THE QUAIL
HOW TO RAISE QUAIL FOR PROFIT

Raising quail is a unique and interesting business, combining pleasure with few drawbacks. The quail is easily raised, cost very little to feed, are hardy, healthy and generally free from every contagious disease. The quail brings a better price than all other poultry providing for a decidedly profitable business having a good future before it.

DUCKING DAYS
1919 – An anthology

Narratives of duck hunting by famous outdoorsmen who had the good fortunate to have spent time on lakes, rivers and marshes during the Golden Age of hunting. "A Texas Duck Hunt" "Following the Redheads to the Gulf Coast" "On Missouri River Bars" "Duck Shooting on the Illinois River" more

DUCK SHOOTING AND HUNTING SKETCHES
1916 - William C. Hazelton

Narratives of Duck Hunting Experiences, Habits of Our Wild Fowl and Hunting Methods, Facts Concerning Migration, Breeding Grounds, Food and Articles about Some of Our Game Birds and Several Anecdotes on Hunting Dog Tales of the hunt from the Golden of Age of hunting on by-gone marshes, rivers and lakes.

FISHING AND SHOOTING SKETCHES
1909 – Grover Cleveland

This is a timeless collection of sporting tales by President Grover Cleveland who was both a dedicated hunter and fisherman; an experienced angler and excellent wing shooter. But he knew his shortcomings. On quail shooting, for instance he admitted. "I do not assume to be competent to give advice on shooting. I miss shots too often to undertake such a role."

FUR FEATHER & FIN – *Trout Series*
1904 – Alfred E. T. Watson

Anyone who is desirous of obtaining a fair share of piscatorial good fortune should take care that his fishing garb is sober of hue and not of a nature to attract the attention of the trout. Let your rod be light and gentle, and let not your line exceed three or four hairs at the most; but if you can attain to angle with one hair, you shall have more rises and catch more fish. *Trout Wisdom*

FUR FEATHER & FIN – *Snipe & Woodcock Serie*s
1903 – Alfred E. T. Watson

For the sportsman memories of upland hunts for either bird evokes arguments favoring one over the other. Such is the depth of feelings experienced when seeking sport with these little game birds. Fur Feather and Fin **Snipe & Woodcock Series** first published in 1903 explores the habits, haunts and shooting techniques of these elusive denizens of the uplands.

GAME FARMING
1915 – A Hercules Powder Company Publication

Game Farming provides step by step instructions on the breeding and preservation of quail, partridge, pheasant, wild duck and grouse. Contained in this extensive reference book is information to their natural feed, habitat, the control of natural enemies. It focuses on the need, based on the excesses of unchecked hunting practices for restoration of game through the application of responsible breeding practices.

JIST HUNTING
1921 – Ozark Ripley

"Ozark Ripley loves the outdoors, the far horizons and dogs. And every dog I have ever known loved Ozark. A man who loves dogs and is loved by dogs always rings true." Ozark shares his experiences with rod, gun and old mother earth immersed in the outdoors with only frying pan, a bag of flour, a bit of bacon, a blanket, rushing, streams, wind kissed waters, and woodland trails.

LAKE FIELD AND FORREST
1899 – Frank A. Bates

A wonderful collection of stories by self proclaimed "sportsman-naturalist" Frank Bates. Published in 1899 his stories paint a lavish picture of a golden era of hunting and fishing that thankfully has been preserved through the journals and writings of sportsmen like Bates of that time.

PHEASANT FARMING
A DETAILED "HOW TO"

IN AMERICA we have been very wasteful of our natural our resources. This is especially the case in the destruction of our game birds. That we must produce, if we would destroy has finally dawned on us. Propagation is the only solution of the future game supply problem.

PRACTICAL DRY FLY FISHING
1912 - Emlyn M. Gill

The subject has been fully covered by a number of expert writers who have lived in the home of the dry-fly, England.

With the exception of a few magazine articles, there has been little American Literature upon the subject. This work is confined to the floating fly. The beauties of nature, one of the chief attractions of a day on the trout stream, are left to the poetic pens of English literature.

SCATTERGUN SKETCHES
1922 – Horatio Bigelow

WHEN business binds and you can't seem to get away on that long anticipated shooting trip, you can find relief in the "Call of the Wild". When gathered around the camp-fire how often have you heard the "old timers" spin the yarns that linger with you? These are those yarns from long ago told with wit and an eye for detail which will carry you back.

SPECKLED BROOK TROUT
1902 – Various authors

The brook trout has long held a special place in the hearts and minds of anglers. Lavishly illustrated this volume, a collection from the pens of a number of well known writers, begins by supplying general information on the wily brookie, before moving on to discuss habitat, habits and angling methods then finally culinary considerations.

TALES OF DUCK AND GOOSE SHOOTING
1922 – William C. Hazelton

Whether hunted for food or to show skill with a gun some imperative causes man reject all creature comforts, brave exposure to nasty weather, or risk the danger of accidental mutilation or death. Along with the duck season comes a longing to fondle a gun and sit staring at the ammunition box. This wonderful collection recounts stories from the golden era of water fowling.

THE ART OF WING SHOOTING
1895 – William Bruce Leffingwell

The Art of Wing Shooting is a practical treatise on the use of the shot gun. Illustrated by sketches and easy to read it guides you to become an expert shot. It contains a complete expose of the scientific use of the shot gun along with an examination of the habits and resorts of game birds and waterfowl. And how to become a proficient inanimate target shot.

THE BOYS BOOK OF HUNTING AND FISHING
1914 – Warren H. Miller

"There is but one excuse for the men of to-day and that is to prepare boys by instilling in them an enduring appreciation for the great outdoors; undoubtedly a good thing." This work is devoted to the proper use of rod and gun to provide an opportunity to go to the open for their games and recreation with the helping hand of an exhaustive book on sports of the outdoor world.

THE IDYL OF THE SPLIT BAMBOO
1920 – George Parker Holden

The fisherman's transcendent implement is his rod. While few anglers might undertake making a split cane rod it requires little to convince anyone that fishermen love to tinker with their tackle. If you can make a rod you certainly can fix one. Building a split-bamboo rod is an operation in overcoming those particular difficulties in handling and working bamboo which give the most trouble

THE SPORTING DOG
1904 – Joseph A. Graham

It's commonly conceded that Great Britain provided the stock all our dogs of sporting breed. So how do they differ from the British dogs? Reduced to the simplest terms they are faster, lighter and quicker in action."*The Sporting Dog*" is a fascinating study of the development of the American hunting dog.

TRAINING THE HUNTING DOG
1901 – B. Waters

Dog training, considered as an art, has no mysteries, no insurmountable obstacles, and unfortunately no short cuts. It is a result of patient schooling analogous to that employed in the training a child. In this case however the trainees are being prepared for limited service in the pursuit of game. Full of practical, usable, effective training methods it is as relevant today as it was 100 years ago.

TROUT FISHING FOR BEGINNERS
Richard Clapham

The perfect gift for either the beginning trout angler or the seasoned angler who can occasionally use a gentle reminder of how often ignoring the basics of the sport can lead to an empty creel. This is a wonderful little classic that should be a part of every sportsman's library.

TROUT FISHING IN AMERICA
1914 – Charles Zibeon Southard

The author attempts to settle once and for all the raging controversy over whether it is better to embrace the dry fly or wet fly school of fly fishing. And while this topic remains unresolved this classic is a richly warm and extensively useful volume on virtually every aspect of fly fishing for trout. From rod to reel, from line to leader no stone in the stream is left unturned.

THE WILDERNESS HOME
1908 – Oliver Kemp

IF you love the out-of-doors, this book was written for you, to crystallize and bring into reality that vague longing which you have felt for a lodge in the wilderness.

Somewhere the trail has led you to the ideal spot in the deep forest, by the shores of a smiling lake or within sound of the murmuring waters.

WING SHOOTING
1881 – Anonymous

The author in "Wing Shooting" provides full directions for the various methods of loading the modern breach-loader, along with instructions concerning powder, shot and wadding. Also covered are general hints on wing shooting together with instructive and positive methods for hunting snipe, woodcock, grouse and quail.

WOODCOCK SHOOTING
1908 – Edmund Davis

Lazy days spent in the uplands inevitably bring a closer connection with nature; especially when your sport is seeking that wily little game bird, the woodcock. For the woodcock reassures us that the brooks are still dancing merrily through the woods and are on their way to sweet scented meadows. So it is, the woodcock brings joy to the lovers of forest, cover and stream.

Additional sporting title available from
Hand Thrown Books

IF HE'S DEAD NOW HE'LL BE DEAD IN THE MORNING
2012 – J. C. Dougherty

Tales of full creels, full waders and the all too occasional perfect point from a snazzy setter. Revisit with the author crisp autumn days wandering bird-less through the woods, or sunny spring afternoons casting about for un-cooperative trout. These are stories of life-long friends and life-long laughs. Journal of a Somewhat Amusing Outdoor Life is the perfect gift for the sportsman in your life.

AN EDIBLE MEMOIR   2014 - J. C. Dougherty

Where north meets south; from grits to game birds Recipes and tall tales about the big ones that got away and the collard greens that couldn't. Black Eye Pea Fritters with Onion Jam ~ Woodcock Pie ~ Cajun Fried Bullfrog ~ Hush Puppies ~ Fried Grits ~ Duck Soup with White Beans ~ Fried Catfish Southern Fried Chicken ~ Okra Fried to within an inch of its life!

THE ART OF RESTORING SPLIT CANE FLY RODS.
2012 – J. C. Dougherty

Split cane bamboo fly rods are not for everyone, some people are too addicted to high tech. Bamboo rods only warm the heart and are in tune with the rhythms of the rivers streams and lakes they touch. And there's little else that is as satisfying as bringing one of these classic rods back to life. Advice, tips and instructions on how to repair cracks, splits broken ferrules cork grip and more.

Hand Thrown Books

West Newbury, MA
www.handthrownbooks.com

.

www.ingramcontent.com/pod-product-compliance
Lightning Source LLC
Chambersburg PA
CBHW070554290526
45790CB00002B/680